RACIAL JUSTICE IN AMERICA

How Can I BE AN ALLY?

FATIMA D. EL-MEKKI WITH KELISA WING

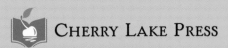

Published in the United States of America by Cherry Lake Publishing Group
Ann Arbor, Michigan
www.cherrylakepublishing.com

Reading Adviser: Marla Conn, MS, Ed., Literacy specialist, Read-Ability, Inc.
Content Adviser: Kelisa Wing
Book Design and Cover Art: Felicia Macheske

Photo Credits: Library of Congress/Photograph by Jack Delano, LOC Control No.: 2017747598, 5;
© Diana Grytsku/Shutterstock.com, 9; © Rawpixel.com/Shutterstock.com, 10; © dotshock/Shutterstock.com, 13; © Daniel
M Ernst/Shutterstock.com, 17; © Iakov Filimonov/Shutterstock.com, 19; © Everett Collection Inc/Alamy, 23; © Monkey
Business Images/Shutterstock.com, 27; © Eugenio Marongiu/Shutterstock.com, 29; © JNix/Shutterstock.com, 30

Graphics Throughout: © debra hughes/Shutterstock.com; © GoodStudio/Shutterstock.com; © Natewimon Nantiwat/
Shutterstock.com; © Galyna_P/Shutterstock.com

Library of Congress Cataloging-in-Publication Data
Names: ElMekki, Fatima, author. | Wing, Kelisa, author.
Title: How can I be an ally? / Fatima D. El-Mekki, Kelisa Wing.
Description: Ann Arbor, Michigan : Cherry Lake Publishing, 2021. | Series:
    Racial justice in America | Includes index. | Audience: Grades 4-6 | Summary: "Race in America has been avoided in
    children's education for too long. How Can I Be an Ally? explores the idea of how people can use their privilege to
    advance the culture of inclusion in a comprehensive, honest, and age-appropriate way. Developed in conjunction with
    educator, advocate, and author Kelisa Wing to reach children of all races and encourage them to approach race
    issues with open eyes and minds. Includes 21st Century Skills and content, as well as a PBL activity across the Racial
    Justice in America series. Also includes a table of contents, glossary, index, author biography, sidebars, educational
    matter, and activities"— Provided by publisher.
Identifiers: LCCN 2020040019 (print) | LCCN 2020040020 (ebook)
    | ISBN 9781534180253 (hardcover) | ISBN 9781534181960 (paperback)
    | ISBN 9781534181267 (pdf) | ISBN 9781534182974 (ebook)
Subjects: LCSH: Multiculturalism—United States—Juvenile literature. |
    Social integration—United States—Juvenile literature. | Social
    justice—United States—Juvenile literature.
Classification: LCC E184.A1 E43 2021 (print) | LCC E184.A1 (ebook) | DDC
    305.800973—dc23
LC record available at https://lccn.loc.gov/2020040019
LC ebook record available at https://lccn.loc.gov/2020040020

Cherry Lake Publishing Group would like to acknowledge the work of the Partnership for 21st Century Learning, a
Network of Battelle for Kids. Please visit http://www.battelleforkids.org/networks/p21 for more information.

Printed in the United States of America
Corporate Graphics

Fatima D. El-Mekki has a Bachelor's degree in Islamic Studies and is the author of five children's
books. She has always been curious about and committed to helping communities develop a deeper
understanding of different cultures and races. Bringing people from different backgrounds, religions,
and experiences together has always been one of Fatima's life and career goals.

Kelisa Wing honorably served in the U.S. Army and has been an educator for 14 years. She is the
author of *Promises and Possibilities: Dismantling the School to Prison Pipeline, If I Could: Lessons for
Navigating an Unjust World,* and *Weeds & Seeds: How to Stay Positive in the Midst of Life's Storms.*
She speaks both nationally and internationally about discipline reform, equity, and student
engagement. Kelisa lives in Northern Virginia with her husband and two children.

CHAPTER 1

Introduction to Allyship

It was 1963, and racial segregation kept Black people separated from White people both legally and socially. They couldn't live in the same neighborhoods, attend the same movie theaters or schools, or play on the same playgrounds. They couldn't use the same restrooms or eat at the same restaurants. City and state officials created laws against Black people just because of the color of their skin. Police were used to enforce those laws. Even though the U.S. Supreme Court had ruled in 1954 that racial segregation in schools was illegal, it was still rampant everywhere else in society.

White people had privileges simply because of their skin color. Many people believed this was unfair and wanted to fight against this injustice.

A segregated train station in Durham, North Carolina.

Diversity

What makes rainbows magical? It's all the different colors that make up the whole. Every color is unique, but when they are next to each other, they create a beautiful arc in the sky. **Diversity** is what makes the world beautiful. The diversity of our skin colors should not be a reason to separate us. It should bring us together.

In April of 1963, the police were called on a group of Black students who tried to attend a "Whites only" movie theater in Baltimore, Maryland. A White man named William Lewis Moore was there and refused to ignore the situation.

Moore stood by the Black students and waited to get arrested along with them. He was a **civil rights activist**, and he wanted to fight against injustice. He had attended multiple civil rights protests and was not afraid to do what he thought was right. He believed that everyone, regardless of the color of their skin, deserved to be treated like human beings. At the movie theater that day, Moore acted on his beliefs of equality and fought for racial justice. He was an **ally** of the Black community.

Racial Justice

It is easier to understand what racial justice is if the words are explained separately. What is race? Usually, when people talk about race, they mean the color of your skin. What is justice? Justice means fairness and equal treatment. For example, if White students can get a great education, justice means that Black students should assume they can get one too. When Black students don't have the same educational opportunities as White students, that is racial injustice. Another example involves criminal behavior. Someone who commits a crime should be punished. But it is unjust if, for the same crime, a White person is not punished while a Black person is. What William Lewis Moore wanted was equality and fair treatment for Black students.

CHAPTER 2

What Is an Ally?

An ally is a helper. An ally can be someone who belongs to a group that is oppressing another group, but the ally stands with those who are being oppressed in order to get justice. When William Lewis Moore stood up for Black people who were being discriminated against, he was being their ally. He joined in the battle against injustice. He made a choice to not be a bystander while Black people were being victimized. He did not tolerate the prejudice he observed and chose to be an upstander. Upstanders are people who do not ignore discrimination and other forms of injustice. Upstanders speak out, support, and assist marginalized groups.

When it comes to race, an ally is a White person who decides to be an upstander and support Black people who are being discriminated against.

Allies are essential to ending discrimination.

We can be different, but we should all have equal rights. It is unfair to discriminate against someone just because of the color of their skin. Each person's skin color is unique and beautiful—and we all have the same rights, no matter what that skin color is.

What type of discrimination have you faced? How did it make you feel?

Who Was William Lewis Moore?

William Lewis Moore was born April 28, 1927, in Binghamton, New York. First, he was an activist for mentally ill people. Later, he became an activist for Black people. He wrote letters to condemn racial segregation and hand-delivered them to White politicians and others in cities such as Annapolis, Maryland, and Chattanooga, Tennessee—often walking long distances between cities in protest. For his final letter-delivery walk, he wore a sandwich board that read, "Equal rights for all and Mississippi or Bust." Moore was shot during that walk. A member of the Ku Klux Klan was suspected of the murder but never charged. Moore was 35. After he died, the letter he had been carrying was opened. He had written, "The White man cannot be truly free himself until all men have their rights."

CHAPTER 3

Being an Ally

To be an ally, you first need to know who you are. What is your identity? Identity is the combination of things that make you the person you are. It includes the color of your skin, your character, your behavior, what you love doing, your hopes, your beliefs, and much more. Other aspects of your identity can come from where you grew up and what has happened in your life.

First, your identity is mostly affected by your closest relatives and the people you have grown up around. Your religious identity can be affected by how often your parents take you to your place of worship. Your racial identity can be affected by how your parents discuss race with you and around you.

Second, you need to know what your affinity group is. This is the group of people from your family, your race, or your culture. Belonging to a certain affinity group can bring some privileges that other affinity groups do not have.

Third, you must decide what is important to you. Where do you stand on issues of unfairness and injustice?

Belonging to the White (Caucasian) affinity group comes with unearned privileges.

Wrong Is Wrong

You can be proud of who you are, but that pride shouldn't lead to the harm of others. Malcolm X, a Black civil rights activist, said, "You're not supposed to be so blind with patriotism that you can't face reality. Wrong is wrong, no matter who says it." He meant that even though there were U.S. laws and government policies supporting discrimination and racism, that doesn't make it right. He also said, "I'm for truth, no matter who tells it. I'm for justice, no matter who it is for or against. I'm a human being, first and foremost, and as such I'm for whoever and whatever benefits humanity as a whole." This means that your pride of self does not give you the right to oppress others.

Lastly, once you know *who you are* and *where you stand*, you will be able to determine if you want to become an ally. If you've decided to be an ally, you will need to have your listening ears open. You will need to talk to members of the marginalized group. And you must listen to what they have to say about their experiences. Sometimes it can be hard to hear other people's truths. Some of their feedback may be about their experiences with you. You will need to listen without judgment or defensiveness. This is the path toward being an ally.

Being an ally is not a one-time job or something to do just for a day. It calls for commitment. Despite how uncomfortable it may feel, being an ally for people of color calls for honesty and consistency. Are you willing to do so?

The Platinum Rule

The Golden Rule says to treat others with respect—the same way you would like them to treat you. But try using the Platinum Rule too. It says to treat others the way THEY want to be treated.

DO THE WORK!

ESSENTIAL QUESTION

How can we be anti-racist?

Becoming anti-racist requires actively working against racism using words and actions. This project-based learning assignment will allow you to practice these skills. Read all the books in the *Racial Justice in America* series. Through each "DO THE WORK!" activity, you will research and put together parts of a larger project that will allow you to grow and help others grow as well.

Part of becoming an ally is changing oppressive systems. For this portion of your project, you are going to identify oppressive rules or practices in your school or community.

Using research, observation, and mathematical skills, create a chart of any oppressive rules or practices that have been unfair to others based on their differences. For example, does the dress code call girls out specifically? Are there rules about hairstyles that single out certain hair types? Once you have identified the rules or practices, offer a suggestion to change it to be more equal and just for all.

For the presentation of your final work, you can create a collage, magazine, podcast, jigsaw puzzle, poem, video, or social media campaign—anything to demonstrate your learning. No matter what you do, just be creative, learn something new, and publicize your work!

CHAPTER 4

How Can I Be an Ally in My Family?

Let's imagine some different scenes. In one, your family is White and is gathered for Christmas. You have a little sister who gets a Black doll as a gift from her aunt. Your cousin says, "We're White! Why did you give her a Black doll to play with? She should have gotten a White doll, since White dolls are more beautiful than Black dolls!"

Or let's say you're sitting around the dinner table. Your brother tells a rude joke about Kamala Harris, a Black woman and the Democratic nominee for vice president in 2020.

Or you might be at a friend's house and hear her parents talk about how Black people are criminals.

As an ally, when you hear comments like these, a bell should ring in your head. It is an alert to the sound of discrimination. This is the type of racial prejudice that is often taught in the privacy of people's homes. And you know this is wrong because you are aware that there is beautiful diversity in the world.

Rallies and other forms of public protests are important ways to stand up for justice. But so is consistently standing up for it in the privacy of our homes and in conversations with friends and families.

Having a conversation with a loved one or grown-up about their prejudices can be really hard. Being an ally is not easy!

James Zwerg was a White college student from Nashville, Tennessee. In 1961, he wanted to join the group of upstanders who were called Freedom Riders. The Freedom Riders wanted Black people to be allowed to ride the same public transportation as White people. They decided to take a bus ride to the segregated South.

Zwerg's parents did not approve of his desire to stand with Black people in this time of racial segregation. They did not want him to get involved.

After much deliberation, Zwerg decided to participate in this nonviolent act of protest to demonstrate his beliefs. He joined the Freedom Riders, showing that he was an ally to the Black community and an upstander fighting for racial justice. His parents were furious and refused to support him—their relationship was never again the same.

Justice

If there is no justice, there will be no peace. Aisha El-Mekki, a civil rights activist from Philadelphia, often says, "True justice will birth peace." No one wants to be treated poorly. People have been working hard throughout history to bring justice. What is good (justice, peace, and equality) should be encouraged, and what is wrong (injustice, discrimination, and racism) should be forbidden.

John Lewis talks with fellow Freedom Rider James Zwerg after facing violence in Montgomery, Alabama.

CHAPTER 5

How Can I Be an Ally at School?

James Zwerg attended Beloit College in Wisconsin. His roommate was a Black man named Robert Carter. They were different, but they became friends. Zwerg was frustrated and disappointed to see how other White students were treating Carter and other Black students. The racist behavior Zwerg witnessed led him to switch schools. He decided to attend Fisk University, a mostly Black college in Nashville. He wanted to experience being a "racial minority." He thought it would help him understand more deeply how Black people may feel. This likely helped him become a stronger ally in the quest for racial justice.

The Panthers

The Black Panther Party was a Black revolutionary political group founded in 1966. They fought for the equalization of Black people. In 1968 a group of allies created the White Panther Party, an anti-racist group meant to help advance the Black Panthers' goals. Its founders were three White people: Pun Plamondon, Leni Sinclair, and John Sinclair. They launched the group after hearing Fred Hampton, a leader in the Black Panther Party, speak about unity in the fight for racial justice.

The three founders wanted White people to support Black people in their struggles for justice. The party had a 10-point program that included these three points:

1. They wanted freedom for everybody.

2. They wanted justice and the end of violence against people all over the world.

3. They wanted free education for everybody.

School is a diverse place that gives us the opportunity to experience racial diversity. Have you ever noticed a White teacher treating a Black student differently than your White peers? Are your White friends nice or mean to kids of other races? If you see someone being treated badly because of race—or for any reason—that is the moment for you to put on your upstander hat. Politely explain that everyone should be treated equally and with kindness. You could even take a step further and create a group that would stand by the racial minority group like the White Panther Party members did.

We all have the responsibility to make our school an enjoyable place to learn and grow. We cannot do it by ourselves—we need help from teachers and other students. Some students join organizations in a show of unity. Others use their voices to speak and write. A group of students who attended Mastery Charter School's Shoemaker Campus in Philadelphia, Pennsylvania, founded Raised Woke, an activist organization. Raised Woke has participated in protests against the criminalization of Black communities, mass incarceration, and inequality in school funding.

Think about your school. Is it a place of diversity and inclusion?
If not, what can you do to change that?

CHAPTER 6

How Can I Be an Ally in My Community?

To be this kind of ally, you must know the struggles that people of color in your community are facing. You can then connect to social organizations or create a blog. You can also write letters to newspapers like Juliette Hampton Morgan did in 1939.

Morgan, a White woman, sent letters to her local newspaper, the *Montgomery Advertiser*, to condemn the horrible injustices she saw on city buses.

During the time of segregation, Black people had to pay their fare at the front of the bus and then exit the bus and re-enter through the back door. Then they could find a seat. One morning, Morgan saw a Black woman pay her fare and exit the bus. But as the woman walked to the back door to re-enter, the White bus driver pulled away, leaving her stranded.

What struggles do people of color face in your community? How might
you be able to bring about change?

Montgomery Bus Boycott

In Montgomery, Alabama, in 1955, Rosa Parks, a Black bus rider, helped start a movement. She was told to give her seat to a White man or else be arrested. Parks stood for justice by sitting—and refusing to give up her seat. She had paid for that seat just like the White man who wanted to take it from her. As threatened, she was arrested.

Because of that unfair action toward her, Black people decided to boycott Montgomery's buses. They did not ride the buses for 381 days! They were united and organized. And their work led to the U.S. Supreme Court ruling that segregation on public buses was unconstitutional.

Historic marker for the Montgomery Bus Boycott. The boycott marks the beginning of the modern civil rights movement.

THE BUS STOP
The Montgomery Bus Boycott

At the stop on this site on December 1, 1955, Mrs. Rosa Parks boarded the bus which would transport her name into history. Returning home after a long day working as a seamstress for Montgomery Fair department store, she refused the bus driver's order to give up her seat to boarding whites. Her arrest, conviction, and fine launched the Montgomery Bus Boycott. The Boycott began December 5, the day of Parks's trial, as a protest by African-Americans for unequal treatment they received on the bus line. Refusing to ride the buses, they maintained the Boycott until the U.S. Supreme Court ordered integration of public transportation one year later. Dr. Martin Luther King, Jr. led the Boycott, the beginning of the modern Civil Rights Movement.

Morgan was shocked and pulled the emergency cord. She insisted that the bus driver stop and let the Black woman get on. This kind of racism exhibited by bus drivers was not a onetime incident. Morgan exposed this racism by not only insisting the bus driver stop, but also writing a letter to the newspaper about it.

In your community, you can help by stopping injustices when you see them, writing to your newspapers and local leaders, or making signs for protests. What other ways can you think of to be an ally in your community?

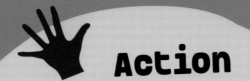

Action

There comes a time when the fight for justice must go beyond talk. People who believe in freedom cannot rest. They must organize, communicate, and walk the talk, not just talk the talk. It means taking action to stop the injustices that are happening, because we want the world to be a better place for everyone.

EXTEND YOUR LEARNING

Celano, Marianne, Marietta Collins, and Ann Hazzard. *Something Happened in Our Town: A Child's Story about Racial Injustice*. Washington, DC: Magination Press, 2018.

Cohen, Miriam. *Layla's Head Scarf*. Long Island City, NY: Star Bright Books, 2009.

Nagara, Innosanto. *The Wedding Portrait*. New York, NY: Triangle Square/Seven Stories Press, 2017.

GLOSSARY

activist (AK-tuh-vist) a person who fights to bring about political or social change

ally (AL-eye) a person who is on the same side as another during a disagreement; a supporter

boycott (BOI-kot) to refuse to buy or use something as a punishment or protest

bystander (BYE-stan-dur) a person present but not involved

civil rights (SIV-uhl RITES) the rights everyone should have to freedom and equal treatment under the law, regardless of who they are

commitment (kuh-MIT-muhnt) the state of being pledged to something

condemn (kuhn-DEM) to disapprove strongly of something

consistency (kuhn-SIS-tuhn-see) the condition of always behaving according to the same principles

discriminated (dis-KRIM-uh-nate-id) treated someone unfairly while treating someone else better

diversity (dih-VUR-sih-tee) a variety

marginalized (MAHR-juh-nuhl-ized) placed in a position of little importance, influence, or power

oppressing (uh-PRES-ing) using power or authority in a cruel and unfair way

patriotism (PAY-tree-uh-tiz-uhm) having strong loyalty to one's country

prejudice (PREJ-uh-dis) an unreasonable and unfair opinion of someone based on the person's race, religion, or other characteristic

racist (RAY-sist) a person who treats people unfairly or cruelly because of their race

segregation (seg-rih-GAY-shuhn) the practice of keeping people or groups apart

unconstitutional (uhn-kahn-stih-TOO-shuh-nuhl) going against the rights given to U.S. citizens in the Constitution

unique (yoo-NEEK) the only one of its kind; unlike anything else

INDEX